AIN'T MISBEHAVIN'

The New FATS WALLER Musical Show

Due to copyright restrictions, the following songs are not included in this book:
Fat 'N Greasy
Your Feet's Too Big
I've Got My Fingers Crossed
Spreadin' Rhythm Around
Two Sleepy People
Viper's Drag/The Reefer Song

Applications for performance of this work, whether legitimate, stock,
amateur, or foreign, should be addressed to:
MUSIC THEATRE INTERNATIONAL
49 East 52nd Street
New York, N.Y., 10022

HAL LEONARD PUBLISHING CORPORATION
Home Office: · National Sales Office:
960 East Mark Street   8112 West Bluemound Road
Winona MN 55987   Milwaukee WI 53213

Cover Art: Doug Johnson
Photography: Martha Swope
Original Cast Recording on RCA
Produced for Records by Thomas Z. Shepard

Ain't Misbehavin'

Words by ANDY RAZAF
Music by THOMAS "FATS" WALLER and HARRY BROOKS

Boy: Tho' it's a fick-le age, With flirt-ing all the rage,

Girl: Your type of man is rare, I know you real-ly care,

Here is one bird with self-con-trol,_ Hap-py in-side my cage.

That's why my con-science nev-er sleeps,_ When you're a-way some-where.

I know who I love best, Thumbs down for all the rest,

Sure was a luck-y day, When fate sent you my way,

My love was giv-en, heart and soul,___ So it can stand the test.
And made you mine a-lone for keeps,___ Dit-to to all you say.

Moderately (♩♩ = ♩³♪)

Chorus:

No one to talk with, all by my-self, No one to walk with, but

I'm hap-py on ___ the shelf, Ain't Mis-be-hav-in', I'm sav-in' my love for

you. ___ I know for cer-tain

'Tain't Nobody's Biz-ness If I Do

Words and Music by PORTER GRAINGER and EVERETT ROBBINS
*Additional Lyric by RICHARD MALTBY, Jr. and MURRAY HORWITZ

Honeysuckle Rose

Words by ANDY RAZAF
Music by THOMAS "FATS" WALLER

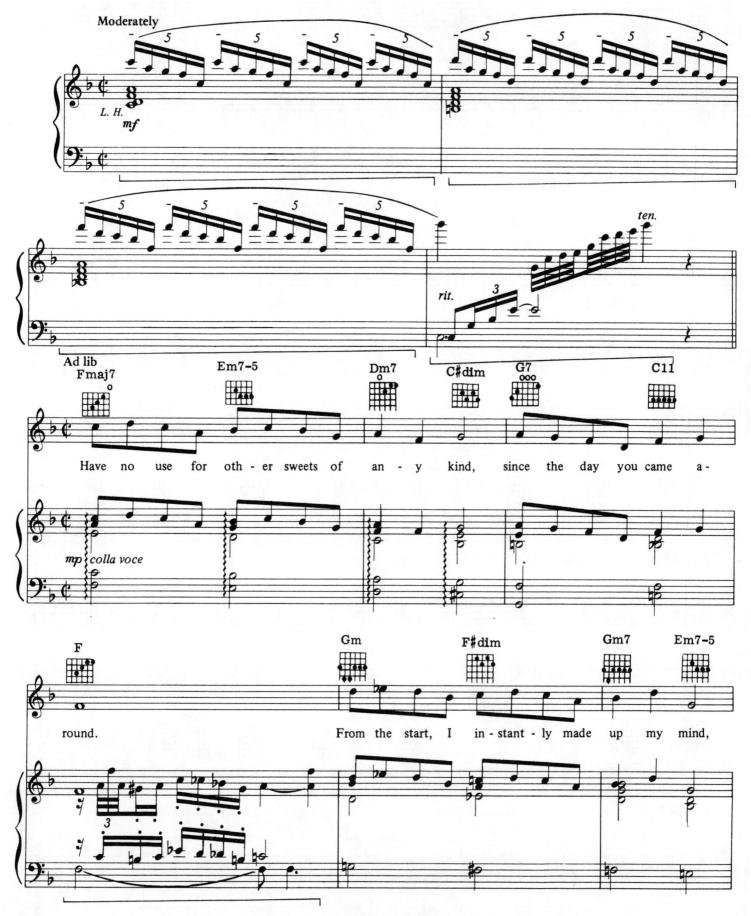

Have no use for oth - er sweets of an - y kind, since the day you came a-

round.

From the start, I in - stant - ly made up my mind,

Lookin' Good But Feelin' Bad

Words by LESTER A. SANTLY
Music by THOMAS "FATS" WALLER

Brightly

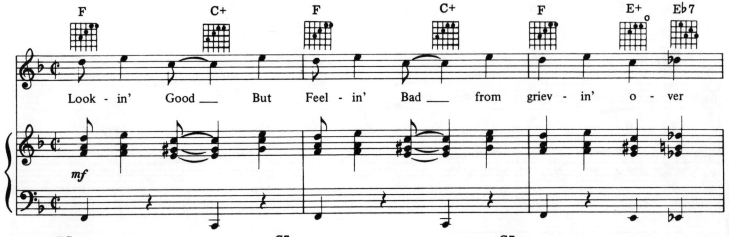

Look-in' Good __ But Feel-in' Bad __ from griev-in' o - ver

you, _____ Look-in' good __ to hide those bit-ter

blues. _____ (Blues. _____) Wea-ry days __ and

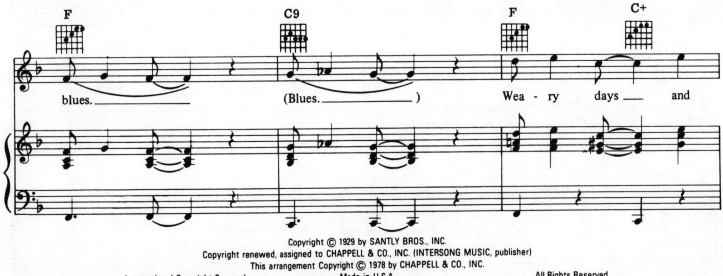

Squeeze Me

Words by CLARENCE WILLIAMS
Music by THOMAS "FATS" WALLER

*Alternate melody on D.S.

Handful Of Keys

Lyric by RICHARD MALTBY, Jr. and MURRAY HORWITZ (based on an idea by MARTY GROSZ)
Music by THOMAS "FATS" WALLER

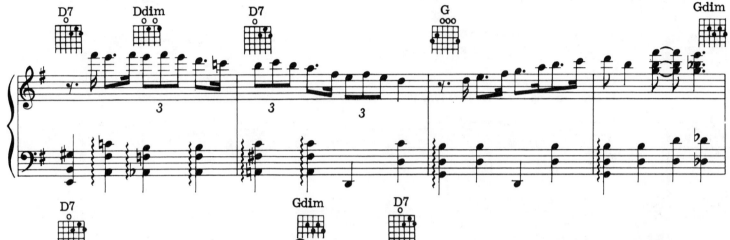

24

27

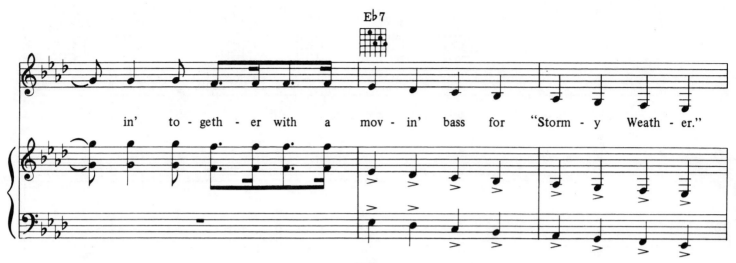

in' to-geth-er with a mov-in' bass for "Storm-y Weath-er."

I____ can nev-er be lone-ly, I got me ev-'ry thing that I please.__

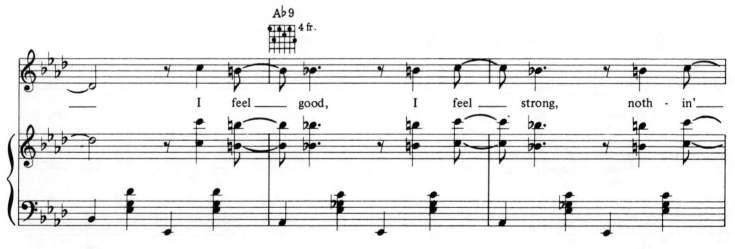

I feel ____ good, I feel ____ strong, noth-in'____

____ bad can go ____ wrong. No-bod-y else com-mands_____ what I

Bang those old eighth notes! Bang those old whole notes!

Stride that old left hand! Rag that old right! There's

such an ap-peal-in', pow-er-ful feel-in', deal-in' with a hand-ful o' keys.

Tacet

Yeah!

L.H.

How Ya Baby

Words by J.C. JOHNSON
Music by THOMAS "FATS" WALLER

The Ladies Who Sing With The Band

Words by GEORGE MARION, Jr.
Music by THOMAS "FATS" WALLER

I've Got A Feeling I'm Falling

Words by BILLY ROSE
Music by THOMAS "FATS" WALLER and HARRY LINK

The Jitterbug Waltz

Lyric by RICHARD MALTBY, Jr.
Music by THOMAS "FATS" WALLER

Slow Jazz Waltz

The night is get - ting on, the band is get - ting slow, the crowd is al - most
I'm tired and out of juice, and yet from head to toe, my bod - y's feel - in'

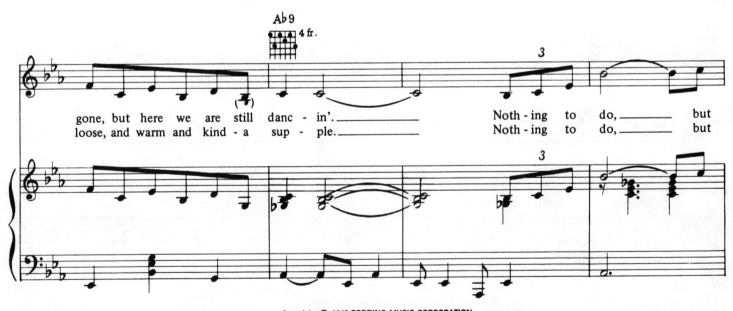

gone, but here we are still danc - in'._____ Noth - ing to do,_____ but
loose, and warm and kind - a sup - ple._____ Noth - ing to do,_____ but

come, let the waltz play a - gain!

The lights have turned to blue, the danc - ers ebb and flow, The room is spin - ning

too, and I'm just mov - ing with 'em,_____ Noth - in' to do,_____ but

waltz. The u - ni - verse has shrunk, there's no - where else to

waltz.

There's noth-ing on my mind, I've reached a new pla-teau, and soon you're gon-na

find a head up-on your shoul-der. Noth-in' to do, but

waltz. It's nice to feel us both get hot be-neath the col-lar.

(Let the ball-room sway.) Where else can you get thrills like this for just a

Yacht Club Swing

Words by J.C. JOHNSON
Music by THOMAS "FATS" WALLER and HERMAN AUTREY

Moderate Swing

Verse:

Ab (C bass)   Bdim   Bb m7   A7-5   Ab maj7

Hoist your an-chor, pull in the plank, hands on ___ deck. ___

Cm7   F9   Bb 7sus4   Bb 7   Eb 7

Strap your life-belt, Read-y Cap-tain, check, dou-ble check. ___

57

When The Nylons Bloom Again

Words by GEORGE MARION, Jr.
Music by THOMAS "FATS" WALLER

Verse:

Gone are the days when I'd an-swer the bell, find there a sales-man with stock-ings to sell, Gleam in his eye, and meas-ur-ing tape in his hand._____ I'd get the urge to go splurg-ing on hose, ny-lons, a doz-en of those! Now, poor or rich, we're en-

59

61

(Get Some) Cash For Your Trash

Words by ED KIRKEBY
Music by THOMAS "FATS" WALLER

63

Off-Time

Words by ANDY RAZAF
Music by THOMAS "FATS" WALLER and HARRY BROOKS

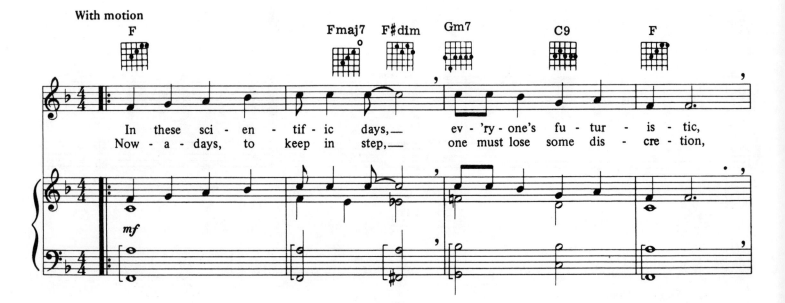

In these sci-en-tif-ic days, — ev-'ry-one's fu-tur-is-tic,
Now-a-days, to keep in step, — one must lose some dis-cre-tion,

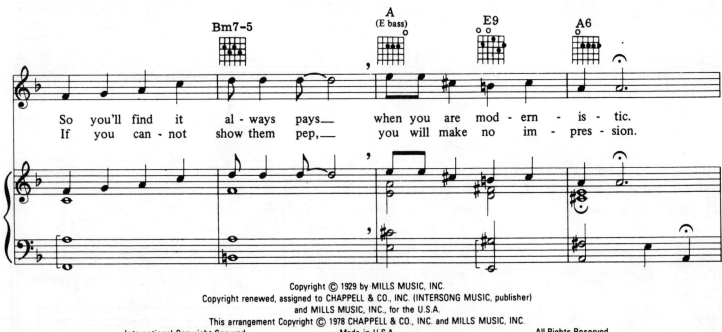

So you'll find it al-ways pays — when you are mod-ern-is-tic.
If you can-not show them pep, — you will make no im-pres-sion.

Lounging At The Waldorf

Lyric by RICHARD MALTBY, Jr.
Music by THOMAS "FATS" WALLER

Mean To Me

Words and Music by ROY TURK and FRED E. AHLERT

The Joint Is Jumpin'

Words by ANDY RAZAF and J.C. JOHNSON
Music by THOMAS "FATS" WALLER

Tempo di-sturb de neighbors

That Ain't Right

Words and Music by NAT "KING" COLE
Additional Lyric by RICHARD MALTBY, Jr. and MURRAY HORWITZ

Slow funky Blues

Ba - by, ba - by, what is the mat - ter with you?

Keepin' Out Of Mischief Now

Words by ANDY RAZAF
Music by THOMAS "FATS" WALLER

87

Find Out What They Like And How They Like It

Words by ANDY RAZAF
Music by THOMAS "FATS" WALLER

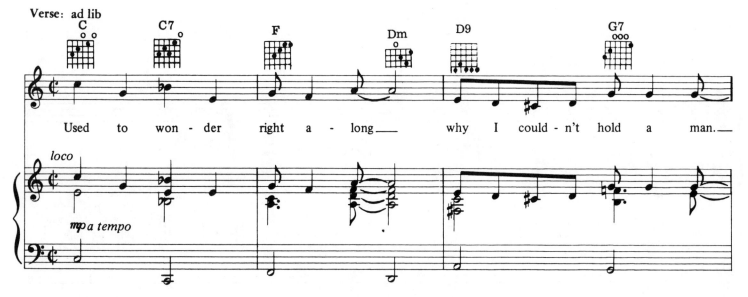

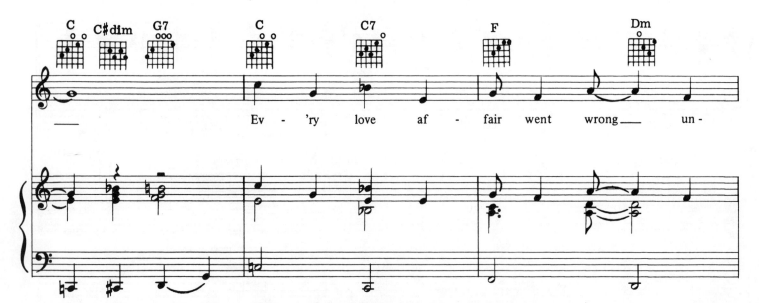

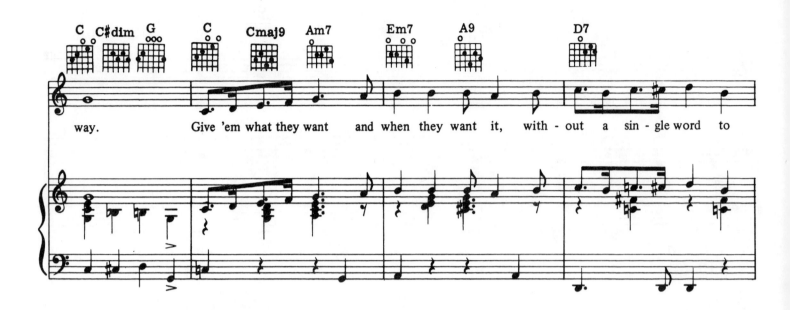

way. Give 'em what they want and when they want it, with-out a sin-gle word to

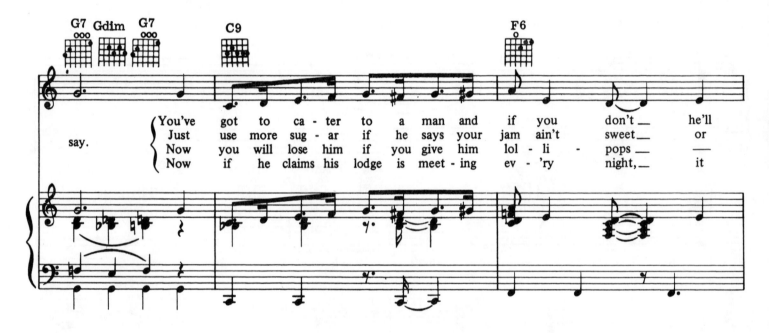

say.

You've got to ca-ter to a man and if you don't ___ he'll
Just use more sug-ar if he says your jam ain't sweet ___ or
Now you will lose him if you give him lol-li-pops ___ —
Now if he claims his lodge is meet-ing ev-'ry night, ___ it

find some oth-er gal to do the things you won't. ___
he will sneak for his des-sert a-cross the street. ___
when you know he's cra-zy just to have some chops. ___
means you do not han-dle all your busi-ness right. ___

Find out what they like, and

(What Did I Do To Be So)
Black And Blue

Words by ANDY RAZAF
Music by THOMAS "FATS" WALLER and HARRY BROOKS

I'm Gonna Sit Right Down
And Write Myself A Letter

Words by JOE YOUNG
Music by FRED E. AHLERT

I Can't Give You Anything But Love

Words by DOROTHY FIELDS
Music by JIMMY McHUGH

Moderately

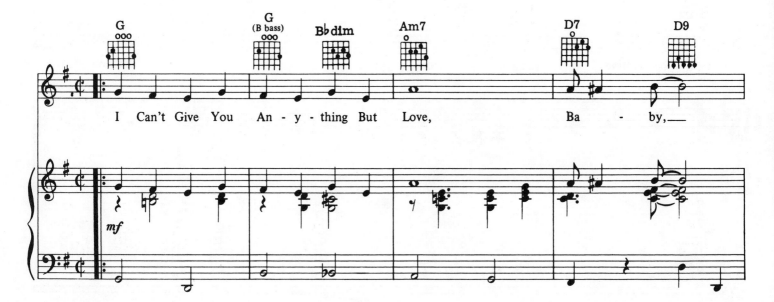

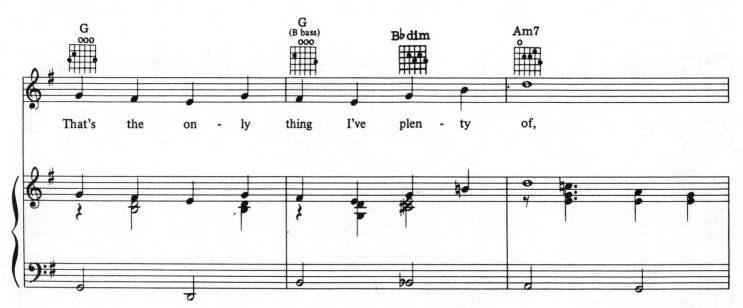

It's A Sin To Tell A Lie

Words and Music by BILLY MAYHEW